Library Technology
REPORTS
Expert Guides to Library Systems and Services

Open Source Integrated Library Systems

Marshall Breeding

Mooresville Public Library
304 South Main Street
Mooresville, NC 28115

ALA TechSource
www.techsource.ala.org

Copyright © 2008 American Library Association
All Rights Reserved.

Library Technology
REPORTS

American Library Association
50 East Huron St.
Chicago, IL 60611-2795 USA
www.techsource.ala.org
800-545-2433, ext. 4299
312-944-6780
312-280-5275 (fax)

Advertising Representative
Brian Searles, Ad Sales Manager
ALA Publishing Dept.
bsearles@ala.org
312-280-5282
1-800-545-2433, ext. 5282

ALA TechSource Editor
Dan Freeman
dfreeman@ala.org
312-280-5413

Copy Editor
Judith Lauber

Administrative Assistant
Judy Foley
jfoley@ala.org
800-545-2433, ext. 4272
312-280-5275 (fax)

Production and Design
ALA Production Services: Troy D. Linker
and Kimberly Saar Richardson

Library Technology Reports (ISSN 0024-2586) is published eight times a year (January, March, April, June, July, September, October, and December) by American Library Association, 50 E. Huron St., Chicago, IL 60611. It is managed by ALA TechSource, a unit of the publishing department of ALA. POSTMASTER: Send address changes to Library Technology Reports, 50 E. Huron St., Chicago, IL 60611.

Trademarked names appear in the text of this journal. Rather than identify or insert a trademark symbol at the appearance of each name, the authors and the American Library Association state that the names are used for editorial purposes exclusively, to the ultimate benefit of the owners of the trademarks. There is absolutely no intention of infringement on the rights of the trademark owners.

ALA TechSource
www.techsource.ala.org

Copyright © 2008 American Library Association
All Rights Reserved.

About the Author

Marshall Breeding serves as the Director for Innovative Technology and Research at the Vanderbilt University Libraries in Nashville, Tennessee. He has authored several previous *Library Technology Report* issues: "Electronic Security Strategies for Libraries," "Strategies for Measuring and Implementing E-Use," "Integrated Library Software: A Guide to Multiuser, Multifunction Systems," "Wireless Networks in Libraries," and "Web Services and the Service-Oriented Architecture." Breeding is also a contributing editor to *Smart Libraries Newsletter*, published by ALA TechSource, and has authored the feature "Automated Systems Marketplace" for *Library Journal* for the last six years. His column "Systems Librarian" appears monthly in *Computers in Libraries* magazine. A regular on the library conference circuit, Breeding frequently speaks at Computers in Libraries, Internet Librarian, and other professional gatherings throughout the United States and internationally. He is a regular panelist on the LITA Top Technology Trends panel at the ALA Annual and Midwinter conferences. Breeding created and maintains the Library Technology Guides Web site at www.librarytechnology.org. For more information or to contact the author, see http://staffweb.library.vanderbilt.edu/breeding.

Subscriptions

For more information about subscriptions and individual issues for purchase, call the ALA Customer Service Center at 1-800-545-2433 and press 5 for assistance, or visit www.techsource.ala.org.

Table of Contents

Abstract — 5

Chapter 1—Open Source Library Automation: Overview and Perspective — 6
- What Is Open Source? — 7
- Open Source versus Traditional Licensing — 7
- Notes — 11

Chapter 2—The Commercial Angle — 12
- Total Cost of Ownership — 13
- Vendor/Product Independence — 13
- Collaborative Development — 16
- Sponsored Development — 16
- Notes — 16

Chapter 3—Major Open Source ILS Products — 17
- History and Background — 17
  - Koha — 17
  - Evergreen — 18
  - OPALS — 19
  - NewGenLib — 19
- Trends in Open Source ILS Adoption — 19
  - Geographic Impact — 21
  - Licensing and Distribution — 22
- Commercial Support Firms — 22
  - LibLime — 22
  - Equinox Software — 23
  - Media Flex — 23
  - Versus Solutions — 24
  - Index Data — 24
- Technology Components — 24
  - Server Operating System — 24
  - Web Server — 24
  - Database Engines — 24
  - Programming Environment — 25
  - Client Environments — 25
- Standards — 26
- Features and Functionality — 26
  - The Scope of the ILS — 27
  - Support for Consortia — 28
  - Online Catalog — 28
  - Circulation — 29
  - Cataloging — 29
  - Acquisitions — 30
  - Serials Control — 31
- Note — 32

Chapter 4—Conclusions and Observations — 33

Abstract

For at least the last two decades, libraries have overwhelmingly obtained their core automation systems from specialized vendors who offer the software through licenses that allow the company to retain exclusive access to the underlying source code. In recent years, open source software has become an increasingly popular alternative. The underlying program code is made available for anyone to inspect, repair, or improve. The open source software movement has entered the library automation industry, introducing a new set of integrated library systems and a clique of companies offering a business model based on service and support rather than software license fees. This issue of *Library Technology Reports* provides an overview of this new aspect of the library automation industry and provides detailed information about the major open source integrated library systems and the companies that support them.

Chapter 1

Open Source Library Automation

Overview and Perspective

This is a time of major transformation in the library automation industry, and the open source software movement has found fertile ground among libraries. Many libraries are moving away from proprietary integrated library systems in favor of open source software. The dynamics of the industry have changed dramatically in recent years—until recently, libraries had largely acquired propriety automation systems from a clique of specialized vendors following the traditional software licensing models. The open source movement has disrupted long-established patterns, introducing a new way of thinking about the development and distribution of software, new products, and a new set of companies seeking to compete against the status quo.

In this issue of *Library Technology Reports* we provide extensive information about the emerging open source software movement as it applies to integrated library systems. As libraries make decisions about what software to use when automating their operations, it is vital for decision-makers to have a solid grasp of the available options. In the past, our options were differentiated on the basis of features, functionality, price, and performance of the software and on the perceived ability for a given company to develop its products into the future and provide adequate support. Do these factors differ with open source ILS products? As we explore open source software, we hope that readers will become well equipped to make informed decisions regarding whether or not this approach benefits their library.

The marketing efforts of the companies involved in open source software evangelize its benefits, while the incumbent companies warn of its dangers. We must look beyond the marketing for the most objective information on this complex issue. On discussion lists and blogs, opinions flow in all directions on the role of open source software in libraries. This report is not meant to advocate for or against the open source approach, but rather to describe in some detail what is different about the open source approach and to provide information about some of the products and companies involved. Readers can then draw their own conclusions.

This report focuses on open source issues specifically relating to integrated library systems. We will provide some general information about open source software and its use in other domains in order to provide some background for the discussion.

ILS in a Nutshell

The Integrated Library System, or ILS, provides computer automation for all aspects of the operation of a library. These products are generally organized into modules that address specific functional areas. Standard modules include cataloging for creating bibliographic records that represent works in the library's collection, circulation that automates tasks related to loaning items to patrons, serials control for managing periodicals and serials, acquisitions to handle the procurement process for new items added to the collection, and the online public access catalog to allow library users to search or browse through the library's collection. Each of these modules offers a very detailed suite of features to accommodate the complex and nuanced routines involved in the library work.

Integrated library systems rely on databases shared among the functional modules. The bibliographic database stores descriptive information about each work in the collection, ideally consistent with the MARC21 standard. A database of authority records ensures consistent forms of names and subject terms and provides references to related terms. Another database tracks information about each item, linking each record for a copy to the appropriate bibliographic record. A patron database manages data for each registered library user. The acquisitions module relies on multiple databases in support of procurement-related functions such as vendors, orders, invoices, and funds. The circulation module involves transactions linking patron and item records when an item is checked out and unlinking them when it is returned. A set of configuration tables, built according to the library's policies on the loan period for each type of material and category of borrower, controls the behavior of the circulation module. The online catalog draws from almost all of the databases and policy tables to provide an interface for library users that enables them to locate items in the library's collections and take advantage of other services offered by the library.

A number of standards have been developed to ensure interoperability among library automation components and to allow the interchange of data. These standards include Z39.50 for the search and retrieval of bibliographic information; SRW/U, a variant of Z39.50 expressed as a Web service; MARC21 for the structure of bibliographic records; AACR2 for consistent syntax for each field within bibliographic records; MARC holdings to represent the issues held for each serial or periodical title; SI for circulation related functions; and P2 or NCIP (NISO Circulation Interchange Protocol) for standard messaging and transactions.

Almost all libraries in the developed world make use of an ILS. In the United States, only very small public or academic libraries, often in rural communities, operate without them.

Some of the major proprietary ILS products currently available include Symphony from SirsiDynix, Millennium from Innovative Interfaces, Aleph from Ex Libris Group, Voyager from Ex Libris Group, Polaris from Polaris Library Systems, Library.Solution from The Library Corporation, Carl.X from The Library Corporation, Spydus from Civica, and many others. The proprietary products have been available for many years, have reached a high level of maturity, and remain the dominant approach used for library automation.

What Is Open Source?

Open source software is free software. It's not necessarily cost-free, but is free to use, free to modify, and free to share. It's a model of dealing with software that presents an alternative to the commercial licensing that imposes many layers of restrictions.

> Please note that the term *free software* tends to be used synonymously with *open source software*. In this report we will use *open source software* since it tends to be used a bit more widely in the library community. All of the ILS products in this space promote themselves as open source rather than free software.

The open source software movement is one of the major alternatives for professionals who work with computer software. On one level, it involves a specific set of software license terms that specify who gets access to the source code that underlies programs, who can change them, what can or must be done with changed versions of the software, and other issues related to modifying the program. But open source also stands for a broader philosophical approach to software that aims to give its users more freedom and allow them to break free from constraints associated with the traditional proprietary model.

Open source software has been a growing part of the overall landscape for the last decade or so. In the broader information technology arena, open source software alternatives have become well-established in key areas of infrastructure from operating systems to web servers. Open source operating systems include many varieties of Linux that compete with proprietary systems like Microsoft Windows. The classic polemic casts Microsoft as a monopolistic domineering company against the open source alternatives that free the world from its stranglehold. In the real world, many individuals continue to choose the proprietary option, and others prefer open source alternatives. These two approaches coexist in the market.

In almost all aspects of computer infrastructure, open source and proprietary software are both available. Table 1 lists some well-known examples of open source and proprietary products available in several categories of computing infrastructure and applications.

Whether a library uses an open source ILS or not it may make use of open source software in other parts of its computing environment.

Open Source versus Traditional Licensing

Open source software is governed by a family of software licenses that embody a philosophy of software freedom,

Category	Closed Source Examples	Open Source Examples
Server operating system	Windows Server 200x	Linux variants (Red Hat, Ubunto, Debian, SUSE Linux)
Database engines	Oracle, DB2, Windows SQL Server	MySQL, PostgreSQL
Programming languages	Microsoft C++	Perl, PHP, Ruby, Python
Desktop operating system	Windows Vista / XP; Mac OS X	Linux + desktop environments (e.g., GNOME or KDE)
Web server	Microsoft Internet Information Server	Apache
Web browser	Microsoft Internet Explorer	Firefox, Mozilla, Opera, Chrome
Office productivity	Microsoft Office	Open Office

Table 1
Common open source infrastructure components

appropriate attribution, and ensuring that no one has an unfair advantage. No single set of rules applies to all—many different flavors of open source licenses have emerged to accommodate many different business models, legal concerns and philosophical standards.

The label *open source* refers to a key principle—that the source code for the software must be made available to its users. Programmers write software using languages like C, C++, Java, or Perl. The code written by the programmer will usually be compiled into a binary form that can be run on a computer. It is this binary form that is most commonly distributed for use, even with open source applications. Distributing the binaries saves the user from the work of recompiling the software and makes for a much easier process of installation.

An Explanatory Note

In some programming environments, the discussion of source code versus binaries will not apply. Programs written in interpreted languages such as Perl, PHP, and JavaScript exist only as source code and are dynamically converted into binary machine instructions upon execution. Some environments compile Perl scripts into a binary form for faster execution, bringing back the distinction. Programs written in C or C++ must be compiled into binary form before they can be installed and executed.

The binary form of the software, while it runs well on a computer, cannot be read or understood by a human. In order to read, understand, and modify code, a programmer needs access to the original source code from which the binaries were created.

In the realm of proprietary software, only the binary form of the program is distributed to users. The original source code is held as confidential proprietary information, made available only to programmers of the organization that created the software application. In a business model that is dependent on revenue from licensing fees and prohibits use by anyone not paying for the product, it's important to control access to the source code, lest unauthorized versions become freely available. In this realm, the way the software works as expressed in the source code is usually a closely guarded trade secret.

In contrast, open source software requires that the source code underlying a computer program be made available to its users. With the source code available, other programmers can study how the software works, fix errors, and make modifications. If the software isn't exactly suited for a given use, it can be adjusted or improved.

The open source model of software development values the inspection of the source code by other programmers. It proposes that when more programmers have the ability to view and study the code, the more likely it is that errors will be discovered and repaired.

The open source approach does not necessarily require that the source code be distributed automatically to each user. The vast majority of users are not programmers and will never have need for the source code. The open source approach requires, however, that there be a convenient way to access the source code on request, even if only binary versions are routinely distributed. In practice, it's common for the download page of an open source application to offer binaries for each of the common hardware platforms or operating systems, with an additional option to select a version that also includes the source code. Some distribution sites offer downloads only for binary versions, with a notice that the source code can be obtained through an e-mail request. Open source software can also be distributed on media like CD or DVD.

Many open source software applications make use of other open source components. A common approach involves LAMP: Linux, Apache, MySQL, and Perl (or PHP). These components form the basis for many open source products. The requirement to make the source code available extends to the prerequisite components. Most open source developers avoid the use of any proprietary components. It is allowable, however, to mix open source and proprietary components under some of the open source licenses. Many commercial proprietary software products, including integrated library systems, make use of open source components.

Open source software, with its inherent requirement for access to source code, comes with the freedom to make changes or derivative versions. If a programmer wants to make changes to an application, it is permissible to do so under any of the open source licenses.

The freedom to modify open source software introduces some complexities related to version control. Ideally, if a programmer discovers an error or makes an improvement in an open source program, those changes can be attributed to the individual or organization that oversees the development of that application and incorporated into future releases and distributions. As more users of the software make more improvements, the application grows in functionality and stability over time. The community of programmers involved in using and improving the software often forms some kind of organization that deals with issues of quality assurance, testing, and version control and might establish a road map for future development.

Another requirement for open source software is the freedom to share. If I have access to an open source software application, I can share it with someone else. If I modify the software, I'm free to share that modified version, provided that I meet certain requirements like giving proper attribution to the original version and making available the source code associated with the modified version. Open source software precludes users from passing off someone else's work as their own. While any user

> The Free Software Foundation offers a definition widely accepted within the open source software community:
>
> Free software is a matter of the users freedom to run, copy, distribute, study, change and improve the software. More precisely, it refers to four kinds of freedom, for the users of the software:
>
> - The freedom to run the program, for any purpose (freedom 0).
> - The freedom to study how the program works, and adapt it to your needs (freedom 1). Access to the source code is a precondition for this.
> - The freedom to redistribute copies so you can help your neighbor (freedom 2).
> - The freedom to improve the program, and release your improvements to the public, so that the whole community benefits (freedom 3). Access to the source code is a precondition for this.
>
> A program is free software if users have all of these freedoms. Thus, you should be free to redistribute copies, either with or without modifications, either gratis or charging a fee for distribution, to anyone anywhere. Being free to do these things means (among other things) that you do not have to ask or pay for permission.[1]

Issue	Proprietary Software	Open Source
Source code	Not distributed to customers.	Available to anyone that uses the software.
Form of software distributed	Binaries / object code only.	Binaries and source code. In some cases, only the source is distributed. If binaries are distributed, source must be available on request.
Who can make changes?	Only the original developer or designates.	Anyone that uses the software.
Sharing—redistribution	Users may not share, resell, or further distribute software.	Users may share the software.
License scope	Licenses apply to a specific product.	Generalized: must not be specific to a given product.

Table 2
Major open source principles

of an open source program is allowed to share derivative versions, there is no requirement to do so.

Open source and proprietary software represent two ends of a spectrum of options (see table 2). Other license variants that fall between these extremes represent a compromise between the two. Some companies and organizations have specific concerns that prevent them from using a completely free approach.

Open source software is not synonymous with "public domain" software. Copyrights apply to open source software, whereas *public domain* generally implies no claim to copyright. Given the implied nature of copyrights, saying that software is in the public domain does not ensure the protections given by open source software licenses.

The Free Software Foundation uses the term *copylefted* for software whose license specifies that no additional restrictions can be added when new versions are created and distributed. Open source software can also be non-copylefted, meaning that it is possible to add some restrictions as it is redistributed. With non-copylefted software, the original free version may be compiled and distributed only as a binary. The original version remains free, but the modified version may not be.

In recent news, open source licenses have been upheld in court rulings. According to Lawrence Lessig, the Court of Appeals for the Federal Circuit ruled that breaking the terms of restrictions specified in an open source license amounts to copyright infringement. This ruling reinforces these licenses as legally binding agreements.[2]

Open source programs adhere to a variety of different licenses. Two of the most popular are the GPL General Public License and the Apache Software License, but there are many widely used alternatives in the field. Each of these licenses has evolved over time. The GPL Public License, given its adoption by all of the Open Source ILS projects, is of particular interest to this report. The Apache license tends to be used more with proprietary commercial software that uses open source components internally. Many of the proprietary ILS products make use of the Apache license for their internal open source components.

Full terms of the GPL General Public License
www.fsf.org/licensing/licenses/gpl.html

Full terms of the Apache Software License
www.apache.org/licenses/LICENSE-2.0.html

The GNU General Public License, now in Version 3, is a full copyleft license that requires software to be free to use in any way, share, and modify. It requires that the source code be made available.

The GNU GPL does not prohibit commercial activity. For instance, you can charge a fee to allow someone to download copies of the software. You cannot require that others charge for downloading or pay you anything if they share it. Charging for downloading GNU GLP software is rare in practice, given that there are always ways for others to get the software without paying a fee. As we will see later, many companies do find business models surrounding open source software. The opportunities for income rely more on value-added services related to the software rather than for basic access to or use of the software itself.

The Apache Software License offers terms more amenable to commercial use. While it is a free license, and compatible with GPLv3, it allows for open source software to transition to a proprietary model. The Apache license does not require that changed versions of an open source software program be distributed under the same terms as the original version. It is possible for the changed version not to be distributed as open source, free software. The Apache Software License allows open source components to be incorporated into proprietary software, provided that certain requirements regarding attribution and licenses notices are met.

The Apache Software Foundation supports the development of some of the most commonly used infrastructure components, like the Apache web server, the Lucene search engine, the Solr search server, the Apache Tomcat Java Servlet environment, and many others.

Apache components are very widely adopted throughout the IT industry. According to Netcraft, the Apache web server ranks as the most widely used web server (49.49%). The proprietary Microsoft Internet Information Server comes in second with 34.88%.[3]

Open Source Initiative
www.opensource.org

Apache Software Foundation
www.apache.org

Free Software Foundation
www.fsf.org

GNU General Public License
www.gnu.org/copyleft/gpl.html

Notes

1. Lawrence Lessig, "Huge and Important News: Free Licenses Upheld," Lessig.org website, Aug. 13, 2008. www.lessig.org/blog/2008/08/huge_and_important_news_free_l.html (accessed Sept. 22, 2008).

2. Netcraft, "August 2008 Web Server Survey," Netcraft website, Aug. 29, 2008. http://news.netcraft.com/archives/web_server_survey.html (accessed Sept. 22, 2008).
3. From "The Free Software Definition," Free Software Foundation website. www.fsf.org/licensing/essays/free-sw.html [accessed Sept. 22, 2008].

Chapter 2

The Commercial Angle

Open source software does not preclude commercial activity. This software generally uses a different business model than traditionally licensed software. The traditional arrangement for a company involves a license with terms that state the amount to be paid for the use of the software, plus additional fees to be paid annually for ongoing support and maintenance.

Companies involved in open source software focus on a different business model, based more on service and other values they can add to the environment. In an environment where libraries can obtain the software itself for free, the business opportunities are usually in providing services libraries will be willing to pay for.

In most cases, companies involved in open source software compete in an environment that includes no-cost options. Red Hat, for instance, bases its business largely on the Linux operating system, which anyone can download and use for free. It's possible to download the software, compile, and configure it for almost any hardware platform around, and yet it's a technical challenge beyond the everyday computer user. Red Hat bases its business on creating a version of Linux that can be easily installed and optimized for different needs, with strong security features and other appealing tools. More importantly, it comes with support. If something goes wrong, the company will provide any needed assistance. For businesses to rely on Linux for their critical infrastructure, they require a high level of confidence in reliability, performance, and quality of service.

The same issues apply in library automation. Any library can download and install open source ILS products like Koha and Evergreen without paying a penny. No library can be denied use of the software. If a company wants to earn revenue from the software, it must offer services that enhance the value of the software enough to provide an incentive for libraries to pay for them.

The services involved in the support of open source software might include some of these:

- **Conversion services.** Whether the process involves automating for the first time or migrating from an existing system, data must be prepared and loaded into the new ILS. For initial automation, retrospective conversion involves creating a database of bibliographic records that corresponds to the library's collections. For libraries with an existing automation system, the process of migration involves extracting all types of data from the incumbent system so that the data can be loaded into the new one. In the ILS arena, library standards like MARC21 ensure the ability to migrate bibliographic data. The ILS includes many other data components not covered as thoroughly by standards that require complex work for both the extraction and loading process.
- **Installation.** A company involved in the support of an open source ILS will offer the software ready to use and thoroughly optimized for the library's hardware. This saves the library from having to download, compile, and install the software and all its prerequisites.
- **Configuration.** Preparation of an ILS for the use of a library can be a complex and tedious process. An ILS is a highly parameterized system, and it's necessary to provide a complete description of the way that the library will use the system. This information must be properly coded into the configuration and policy tables of the system.
- **Training.** The ILS impacts almost every aspect of the operations of the library and requires almost all

Open Source Integrated Library Systems **Marshall Breeding**

staff members to be familiar with its use. Anytime a library changes to a new system, a large portion of the effort involves teaching library personnel how to use the components of the system necessary for them to carry out their work. One of the key services that can be provided by a company involved in an open source ILS involves training sessions delivered by experts in the use of the system.

- **Ongoing support.** Once the library puts the software into production, operations depend on its reliable performance. Any problems with the software can have a negative impact on the library's services. Support contracts provide the library with technical assistance and expert advice on the use of the system as needed. If the library discovers a bug in the software or if the software fails to perform in some way, the company providing the support is expected to resolve the issue. Without ongoing support, the library incurs a degree of risk that problems could arise that it could not resolve on its own.
- **Hosting.** Many libraries prefer the software-as-a-service (SaaS) approach, where the vendor hosts the application. With SaaS, the vendor provides the hardware and assumes responsibility for the installation, configuration, and maintenance of the software. The business model for SaaS generally involves an annual subscription fee that covers the hosting and maintenance of the software. This approach saves the library from having to purchase its own hardware for the server and obviates the need for technical staff to perform system backups, server administration, security patches, and other tasks related to the technical upkeep of the ILS.
- **Custom development.** If the software does not have a specific feature that a library needs, it might choose to engage a vendor to enhance the software. In the open source model, these enhancements can be contributed back into the software so that other users also benefit.

We should note that these services correspond to those that we would expect from a vendor offering proprietary software. With proprietary software, some of these services may be bundled into the license fee, which authorizes the library to make use of the software.

Total Cost of Ownership

An important question related to the adoption of an open source ILS is whether it results in lower or higher cost to the library. The proponents of open source make claims that their approach results in substantial savings to a library over time. Companies involved with proprietary software dispute those claims. There may be no simple answer to that question. It's up to any library deliberating between open source and proprietary solutions to perform its own analysis of which approach is most cost-effective given the library's circumstances and expectations. Considering just the cost issues, setting aside philosophical preferences, quality, and functionality of software, it's important to work out the total cost of ownership for the solution for as many years as the library plans to use the software. Given that a typical library will operate an ILS for 10 to 15 years (provided that the company stays in business and the product remains viable), the total cost of ownership should be calculated over at least a 5- to 7-year period.

Table 3 describes some of the major categories of cost involved in the implementation and operation of an integrated library system, highlighting some of the factors that differentiate open source and proprietary systems.

Vendor/Product Independence

A common argument in favor of open source software is that it gives users more support options and less vulnerability to business transitions. In the proprietary software arena, if a company goes out of business or is acquired by a competitor, then the ongoing viability of that product can be jeopardized. Without the development and support of the original vendor, the product will stagnate, and the libraries that use it may have to migrate to another product. In the case of a business acquisition, the new owners of the software may or may not choose to continue development and support of the products involved. It also may not be possible for another company to step in to take over development and support. If the company that originally developed the software does not provide good service or decides not to continue developing or supporting it, the libraries using that software cannot go somewhere else. With propeitary software, a product remains closely connected with the company that owns and controls it.

In the open source realm, the connection between a software product and a given company is more flexible, at least in theory. Although a company may spearhead the development of a product, once the product is released as open source, a more diffuse body of programmers can become involved. If the company goes out of business, any other interested company, individual, or organization can step in and provide development and support. At any time, multiple companies can provide support for the same product. If a company fails to provide good support, the users of the software can engage another.

We see different examples of multi-vendor support in the open source ILS arena. Koha was originally developed

Cost	Open Source	Proprietary
Technical Infrastructure		
Personnel: server administrator	Neutral cost impact when comparing open source and proprietary options. Under either approach, some support contracts may include full support for server and operating system, obviating the need for a local server administrator. Cost = x FTE * Salary * total years of ownership.	
Personnel: applications programmer	Possible higher need with open source ILS.	Large organizations may employ an applications programmer to work with the ILS. Most small to mid-sized installations do not require an applications programmer to work with the ILS.
Server facilities: personnel, monitoring equipment, data center, racks, etc.	Neutral cost impact. For local installations of either open source or proprietary ILS, the library or its parent institution will need to house the ILS server in its data center. This may involve start-up costs and ongoing annual costs related to the personnel and operational cost of the data center. Total cost of these facilities involves any up-front costs in preparing the data center, plus an allocation for each year of ownership of the system that includes a portion of the cost of operating and staffing the data center.	
Server facilities: cooling, power	Significant costs in maintaining a local installation of either software model. Involves the cost of redundant uninterruptible power, cooling equipment, and energy costs. Must be factored in for each year of ownership.	
Licensing Fees		
License purchase for base system and required modules	Not applicable to open source software.	License fees generally assessed according to the size and complexity of the library.
License fees associated with prerequisite components (Oracle, etc.)	Most open source products do not involve licensed components.	License fees may apply to the operating system, database engines, and other components. These licenses fees may include both up-front costs and annual payments.
Software Support		
Software maintenance for access to upgrades and enhancements	No annual license fees, but no guarantees that new versions of the software will be produced.	A component of annual maintenance supports extensions of the duration of the license and access to new versions of the software. Must be factored for each year of ownership.
Software support for assistance with functional questions or to resolve software or hardware failures	Contracting with a vendor for support services is optional, but a practical necessity for most libraries. Given that most of the income to the vendor concentrates in this category, libraries may expect higher fees in this area to offset lack of licensing fees. Support costs must be factored for each year of ownership.	Annual support for support services bundled into annual fees. Is usually mandatory. Many vendors offer different service levels with corresponding pricing. Must be factored in for each year of ownership, including possible adjustments for inflation.
Systems librarian to manage the ILS: local support and training, policy maintenance, data loading, reports, customization, problem solving	Neutral cost impact. The need for a systems librarian is more a factor of the size and complexity of the library than the license model. Mid-sized to large libraries will employ a systems librarian who devotes significant attention to the ILS, among other responsibilities. Large libraries tend to have multiple systems librarians. Must be factored in for each year of ownership.	

Table 3
Cost factors: open source vs. proprietary

Cost	Open Source	Proprietary
Start-up Costs		
Retrospective conversion	For first-time automation projects, the library will need to build a database that represents its collection. One-time start-up cost.	
Data extraction from legacy system	Libraries converting from a legacy system will need to create routines that extract data of all types from the system: bibliographic, holdings, item, circulation transactions, patrons, orders, vendors, funds, system history, etc. One-time start-up cost.	
Data conversion	Data from the legacy may need to be transformed into a different format for the new system. One-time start-up cost.	
Software installation	The installation of the software onto the library's hardware can be performed by the library itself, or it may include this task as part of a contract of services from a vendor.	While some proprietary vendors allow self-installation, most require the installation to be performed by its authorized representative, which is often covered in the software license fee.
ILS policy configuration	The process of fully configuring the ILS with all of the policies and preferences of the library is proportional to the size and complexity of the library and can represent a large investment of personnel time. Both proprietary and open source vendors offer support options to take on more of this work and reduce the library's time investment.	
Testing / acceptance	Neutral cost impact. The typical installation process involves significant testing of the system by staff throughout the library to ensure that the system functions as expected prior to making the transition to production use.	
Training		
IT and systems staff for technical maintenance	IT personnel and library systems staff must be trained on the technical operation of the software, including configuration and customization details, system tuning options, backup procedures, report creation, diagnostics, troubleshooting, and problem resolution. Mostly a neutral cost impact. Either licensing model may involve options that reduce the library's technical involvement in operating the ILS.	
Library staff members on functional modules appropriate to their job responsibilities	Neutral cost impact. Regardless of licensing option, all staff must receive detailed and extensive training on how to operate the system for the functions within their areas of responsibility. Vendors involved in both licensing models offer training services. Libraries should also plan for training in subsequent years of operation for new staff members and for any necessary refresher courses.	
Software-as-a-service	Vendors involved with both licensing options offer their respective products in a software-as-a-service model, in which the vendor hosts the software. Libraries access the software via the Internet. This model dramatically alters many of the above cost considerations. SaaS generally involves a monthly or annual fee that covers a large portion of the costs mentioned above. For proprietary systems, the monthly SaaS subscription fee will also include the licensing fees, and may obviate the large up-front license payment. The SaaS option involves a higher monthly cost at the trade off of reducing or eliminating many of the up-front costs.	

Table 3
Cost factors: open source vs. proprietary *(cont.)*

by a company in New Zealand, Katipo Communications. In the United States and Canada, LibLime markets and provides services for Koha. In France, a company called BibLibre provides Koha-related services. Other companies are emerging in other geographic regions. To date, there are no major examples of multiple companies competing within the same region for the support of an open source ILS.

In practice, each of the companies involved in open source ILS focuses its attention on a single product and generally has fairly exclusive involvement relative to that product. It remains possible that we will see additional competition for support for open source ILS products as this sector of the market expands and matures.

In some ways, the business dynamics of open source vendors is similar to that of proprietary vendors. The geographic distribution of companies offering support for Koha is not unlike the arrangement seen with many vendors of proprietary software, who partner with other companies to market and sell their products in specific countries or regions.

Where regional distributors for a proprietary ILS are arranged through contracts that that assign a company specific rights regarding a product—like marketing and support within a defined area—the proliferation of companies supporting an open source product occurs more informally. If a company intends to become involved in providing services for a given open source product, it does not need to obtain permission to do so.

We have seen some examples where support for a product has shifted from one company to another as the result of business transitions. In February 2007, LibLime made an agreement with Katipo Communications to assume the portion of its business related to Koha, including the support arrangements for the libraries in that region. In July 2008, CARE Affiliates was acquired by LibLime. The contracts made by CARE Affiliates, primarily involving federated search implementations using open source components from Index Data, were assumed by LibLime.

So far, there are no major examples of libraries using an open source ILS and demonstrating vendor independence by moving from one company to another for support. There have been libraries using open source products whose support arrangement was transferred from one company to another as a result of a business transaction. These transfers of support happen regularly in the proprietary ILS arena.

An important part of this issue involves the support and development options that exist with open source software that are not possible with proprietary software. A library can use an open source ILS without direct involvement from any commercial company, and if it wants to contract for support, the library is not forced to work with any specific vendor.

Contracting for services and support for an open source ILS is optional. Many libraries have implemented Koha independently, both within the United States and internationally, including the Delhi Public Library in India, the Nelson Memorial Public Library in Samoa, the Bering Strait and Chinook school districts in Alaska, a group of schools associated with the Southwest Educational Development Center in Utah, the Washington County School District in Utah, and many others.

If the library needs additional assistance beyond what is available within its existing staff, it has many options. It could simply hire its own programmer, or it could contract with a commercial company. Although each of the products has ties to a specific company that specializes in its development and support, a library can hire or contract with anyone it chooses for any services that it might require.

Collaborative Development

With a proprietary ILS, the company that owns the product controls its development. In most cases, development is performed by direct employees of the company. There have been some examples where an ILS company has engaged services from a third-party offshore firm for development, but this has been fairly rare. In general terms, development of a proprietary software product is a closed process.

Open source software allows and even encourages wide participation in ongoing development. Since anyone can gain access to the source code, other programmers can inspect the code, fix bugs, or extend its functionality.

In the current open source sector of the ILS industry, there are companies specializing in services for a given ILS that employ programmers to actively develop their product. Of course, not all development takes place in these companies. Programmers who work for libraries, for other companies, or out of their own interest also contribute to the development of open source ILS products. The open source movement encourages voluntary development efforts, where organizations contribute the equity of their efforts to improve software initially for their own benefit, but ultimately for all users of the software.

Sponsored Development

In the open source ILS arena, the majority of the development of products is performed by their principal support company. One of the key strategies that leads to the improvement of the software involves "sponsored development." As a general principle, each new feature that gets added to the product needs to be paid for only once.

The model of sponsored development has driven the advancement of the open source ILS products. The basic premise holds that open source software components can be paid for only once for the benefit of many. Each library that subsequently adopts the software benefits from the accumulation of features that were sponsored previously. Early adopters bear a larger portion of the costs and assume higher risks, but to the advantage of those that implement the software in a more finished and complete form.

Notes

1. See LibLime press release dated July 28, 2008: http://www.librarytechnology.org/ltg-displaytext.pl?RC=13424. Also based on communications with company officials of CARE Affiliates and LibLime.

Chapter 3

Major Open Source ILS Products

At least four open source ILS products are available today: Koha, Evergreen, and OPALS. (see table 4). While there may be some additional products, these four have emerged as the most widely implemented and serve as good examples of the current state of the art of the open source ILS. While each of these products bears a great deal of similarity in approach, they also differ in features and functionality and in their appeal to different types of libraries This section provides detailed information regarding each of these systems.

History and Background

Koha

Koha claims the status of being the first open source library automation system. This product traces its roots to 1999 in New Zealand, where a group of three libraries, the Horowhenua Library Trust (HLT), needed a new automation system to replace their current library automation system, called Catalist, which was not compliant with the looming Y2K issue. Rather than purchase a commercial system, HLT contracted with a consulting company named Katipo Communications to develop a new Web-based system. They named this new system Koha, the Maori word for gift or donation, and released it as open source, allowing libraries anywhere to use and help develop and support the software. The HLT libraries began using Koha on January 1, 2000.

A fairly quiet period followed the initial release of Koha, with a few individuals and libraries picking up on the system. No groundswell of interest resulted right away. The initial version of Koha was quite adequate for three libraries of HLT that together served a community of about 30,000 residents with a collection of about 80,000 volumes. At that point, Koha did not have some of the features considered mandatory for most libraries—no support for MARC, Z39.50, SIP, or NCIP. It did not seem scalable to handle the load of very large libraries. Nevertheless, the number of libraries interested in Koha continued to increase. Around fall 2000, for example,

Product	Types of Libraries Adopting Product
Koha	Small to mid-sized public libraries, small to mid-sized academic libraries, museums, special libraries. Gradual penetration into libraries of increasing size and complexity.
Evergreen	Consortia of public libraries; individual libraries, especially through SaaS. Increasing interest by academic libraries; next version will address features needed by academic libraries.
OPALS	K–12 school districts, school district consortia, union catalogs, church and synagogue libraries. Primarily deployed as SaaS or large consortial implementations.
NewGenLib	Libraries in the developing world.

Table 4
Open source ILS products and current market profiles

source, Koha then became a starting point available to others to extend. Nelsonville sponsored the development of MARC21, advancing the software to the point where it could be viable for a much broader range of libraries. The Crawford County Library System sponsored the integration of the Zebra XML-based data storage and retrieval into Koha, allowing it to scale to even larger libraries.

Paul Poulain, already involved as a Koha developer in France, was awarded the contract for reworking Koha to support MARC21. Poulain has continued his involvement with Koha and has recently founded BibLibre as a company to provide Koha support and development services in France.

With development of the mandatory components complete, the Nelsonville Public Library began production use of Koha on August 26, 2002, establishing it as the first public library in the United States to rely on an open source ILS. The success of Koha at Nelsonville catalyzed further interest, leading to its adoption by many other libraries and to the formation of LibLime and other firms devoted to its promotion, development, and support.

Evergreen

Another major example of an open source ILS emerged from Georgia. The Georgia Public Library System (GPLS) provides automation support to public libraries throughout the state through a shared library automation environment, called the Public Information Network for Electronic Services, or PINES. Out of the 408 library facilities in the state, at least 266 participate in PINES. These libraries hold a combined collection of 7.7 million items. One of the key tenets of PINES is wide sharing of resources. A single library card entitles a patron of one library to use materials throughout the PINES consortium.[3]

The initial PINES implementation was based on the Unicorn ILS provided by Sirsi Corporation (now SirsiDynix). The initial selection of Unicorn for the PINES was made in 1999, representing one of Sirsi Corporation's largest contracts. The contract for Unicorn extended through June 2005. The PINES project under Unicorn was deployed in two phases, resulting in one of the largest shared automation platforms in the United States.[4]

All was not well, however, as GPLS was not entirely satisfied with the performance of the software and believed that it could develop a new system custom-built to its needs at a lower cost than the fees being paid to Sirsi Corporation. In an open letter dated June 5, 2004, State Librarian Lamar Veatch announced that GPLS had elected to commence the development of its own library automation system.[5] Its review of the options available at that time concluded that none of the products available from the commercial vendors would meet its expectations.

a medium-sized public library such as Nelsonville. The library required support for MARC21 bibliographic records to stay within national standards and to have a path for migrating its database from Spydus. The library participated in statewide MORE resource sharing initiative, requiring support for Z39.50. The library also required SIP2 or NCIP for use with its self-check stations. Koha lacked these features at that time.[1]

Ohio Libraries Share: MORE Statewide Resource Sharing
www.library.ohio.gov/more

In order for Koha to be a viable system for Nelsonville, significant development was required. Rather than looking to a commercial system that might already have these features in place, the library decided to invest in enhancing Koha and issued requests for proposals for specific development tasks. The library estimated that the costs for extending Koha would fall under what it would otherwise have paid for a system from a commercial vendor.[2]

Koha advanced through this sponsored development model. HLT financed the initial development of Koha for its needs as a set of small libraries in New Zealand. Its automation needs were modest, served well by a system with a simple bibliographic database. When released as open

Open Source Integrated Library Systems Marshall Breeding

Beginning in June 2004, a team of programmers at GPLS began a two-year project to develop a new automation system for the PINES consortium. On September 5, 2006, the PINES consortium successfully completed the transition from Unicorn to Evergreen. In the two years since the migration to Evergreen, the consortium has increased its ranks to over 270 library facilities.[6]

As with Koha, the success of Evergreen sparked broader interest. Since Evergreen was built from the beginning to serve a large consortium, it became positioned as a scalable open source ILS. Since the initial launch of Evergreen for Georgia PINES, this open source ILS has continued to build momentum. A company called Equinox Software was formed to promote, develop, and support the product. A growing number of libraries have adopted Evergreen, as we will see below.

OPALS

The Open Source Library Automation System, or OPALS library automation system, was created primarily for the K–12 school library automation market and was open source from its inception. Media Flex, the company behind its development, had previously been involved in creating proprietary ILS products for this library sector. The OPALS software has been in development since about 2000.

The K–12 school library automation market has seen a major transition toward centralized automation at the district level using Web-based systems in the last few years. Having software installed for each individual library within a district, while often a necessity in earlier times, places a high burden on sparse IT resources. OPALS fits well into this model, providing automation at the district level and many larger scale implementations for school district consortia.

The state of New York provides a structure for the support of its nonmunicipal schools, organized into 37 Board of Cooperative Educational Services (BOCES). Of the 721 school districts in the state, all but those in New York City, Buffalo, Rochester, Yonkers, and Syracuse share resources and services through a BOCES. A number of the BOCES in New York have adopted OPALS to deliver library automation and union catalogs for their school libraries. In an even broader initiative, the SCOOLS union catalog was created in support of interlibrary loan services among its participants, based on OPALS software.[7]

The OPALS software emerged from a project in February 2002, where six of the New York BOCES school library systems wanted to collaborate to create a combined resource-sharing environment. This project involved 300 school libraries, 700,000 bibliographic records, and 1.7 million holdings. Initially, the project considered using Koha, but determined at that time that Koha could not scale to a system of this size. A new system was created based on MySQL, Perl, and Zebra and was operational by August 2003. The OPALS decision to use Zebra in combination with MySQL predated the decision to use this combination of database technologies by Koha, which began in December 2005. Media Flex served as the contractor that partnered with the six New York school library systems.[8]

NewGenLib

Interest in open source ILS extends throughout the world. The developing world in particular stands to benefit from finding ways to implement library automation at a lower cost than might be possible through proprietary systems. One effort to create an ILS specifically for libraries in the developing world started in India through a collaboration between a nonprofit professional organization, the Kesavan Institute of Information and Knowledge Management, and a commercial software development firm, Versus Solutions. The development of the software began in about 2003 as proprietary software, but it was released as open source in January 2008.[9]

NewGenLib has not seen adoption in North America. We include it as an example of international interest. Other open source ILS projects in other parts of the world are likely to be underway. If the open source ILS movement in North America can demonstrate lower costs and sustainable support models, we can expect it to have a major impact in the developing world. Many of the library automation projects in the developing world rely on subsidies provided by governmental and nongovernmental agencies. The growth of open source ILS may depend on these agencies moving away from strategies based on proprietary software.

Trends in Open Source ILS Adoption

We're in the early phase of the open source ILS. While some individual libraries began their involvement with these automation systems beginning in about the year 2000, the impact on the overall library automation world has been almost negligible until the last two years. The pioneering efforts of early implementers have led to the creation of viable products and support structures available through commercial companies that make this approach accessible to a broader range of libraries (see table 5).

Companies offering proprietary ILS products have dominated the library automation industry for the last two decades. These products and companies continue to represent a very large proportion of new ILS implementations. When considering the overall installed base of ILSs throughout the world, only a tiny fraction use open source products. Yet, the rate of growth seen in this early

Product	License
Koha	Public libraries (small to mid-sized), small to mid-sized academic libraries, museums, other special libraries
Evergreen	Large-scale library consortia; individual libraries through SaaS
OPALS	School districts; BOCES; individual school, synagogue and church libraries through SaaS
NewGenLib	Libraries in the developing world

Table 5
Open source ILS market trends

phase, if sustained, stands ready to reshape the industry.

According to the most recent "Automation Systems Marketplace" report published in *Library Journal*, LibLime reported contracts for Koha services to 57 libraries in the 2007 calendar year, out a total of 607 for all public and academic libraries, or roughly 9.4 percent. Considering that this was the first year that open source ILS products represented a measurable portion of the market, this figure may represent the beginnings of a major trend.

Date	Library		Branches	Volumes	Population Served
Jan 2000	Horowhenua Library Trust	Catalyst	3	80,000	30,000
Fall 2000	Coast Mountains School District (BC)		8		
Aug 2002	Nelsonville Public Library	Spydus	6	250,000	65,000
Mar 2006	West Liberty Public Library (IA)	Athena	1	18,000	5,000
Dec 2006	Crawford County Federated Library System	Winnebago	10	250,000	88,696
Feb 2007	Hartland Public (ME)	local	1	18,000	6000
Feb 2007	Stow-Munroe Falls (OH)	Dynix	1	120,000	40,000
Aug 2007	INCOLSA	Unicorn	30		
Sep 2007	Central Kansas Library System	various	31		
Oct 2007	Howard County (MD)	Horizon	7	1,000,000	266,000
Jan 2008	Geauga County (OH)	Dynix	7	500,000	85,000
Jan 2008	WALDO Consortium	Voyager	15		
Feb 2008	MassCat Consortium		100		
Mar 2008	Santa Cruz Public	DRA Classic	11	575,000	200000
Mar 2008	Ashtabula consortium	Horizon	6	235,000	
Apr 2008	Northeast Kansas (NExpress)	Unicorn	116		
Jun 2008	Polytechnic University	Data Trek		187,000	
Jun 2008	Salinas Public (CA)	Dynix	3	225,000	150,000
Jul 2008	Highland Park Public (NJ)	Horizon	1	65,000	14,000
Jul 2008	Butte-Silver Bow Public (MT)	Winnebago	1	65,000	35,000
Jul 2008	Grand County Public (UT)	Follett	2	50,000	
Aug 2008	Southeast Kansas	various	11	354,000	
Aug 2008	New Durham Public (NJ)	none	1	12,000	2,500
Aug 2008	Blue Mountains Public (ON)	Winnebago	1		6,500

Table 6
Selected libraries moving to Koha in North America

Date	Library	System	Branches	Volumes	Population Served
Sep 2006	Georgia PINES	Unicorn	270	1,700,000	
Jan 2008	Kent County (MD)	Horizon	3	50,000	20,000
Apr 2008	SITKA Consortium (BC, Canada)	various	18+		
Apr 2008	Michigan Library Consortium	various	6+		
Jun 2008	Marshall Public Library (MO)	Unicorn	1	30,000	12,500
Aug 2008	Indiana Evergreen	various	19	132,000	12,000

Table 7
Selected libraries moving to Evergreen in North America

The announcements made through 2008 presage an even larger proportion. Both LibLime and Equinox Software have made announcements of library commitments to their open source products with greater frequency than seen by the companies offering proprietary systems.

Tables 6 and 7 describe some of the open source ILS projects that have been publicly announced. In some cases, such as SITKA and Evergreen Indiana, the announcement involves an initial phase expected to expand to a much larger scale.

Open source ILS has not yet significantly penetrated the realm of large libraries. In academic libraries, we observe that no ARL (Association of Research Libraries) member has selected an open source ILS. Large municipal libraries have not been moving toward open source products. The King County Library System, a very large library system in Washington, has publicly announced its interest in moving to an open source ILS, with an eye on Evergreen. The Delhi Public Library, a municipal system with 56 branches and a collection of 1.4 million items in India, recently migrated to Koha. It is still unclear the extent to which the Koha system is being used and how that use compares to municipal libraries in North America.[10]

Evergreen has proven itself as a system capable of supporting large library consortia. These consortia tend to be comprised of smaller libraries. PINES, for example, serves over 270 libraries in Georgia, but does not include the high population centers of Atlanta-Fulton County, Cobb County, and DeKalb County.[11]

In broad terms, we can expect the open source ILS products to steadily reach into ever larger library environments as the products mature and become better established. That has been the pattern to date—open source ILS products face the same challenges as proprietary systems in moving into the ranks of larger libraries. Large libraries are reluctant to adopt an ILS that has not already proven itself successful in organizations of similar size and complexity.

Some academic libraries have also begun to move to open source systems. Koha and Evergreen both emerged in the public library sector. Given the differences in automation requirements for public and academic libraries, the question of whether they can be served by the same ILS products is often asked. Koha has demonstrated some appeal to both library types, though its portion of academics remains small relative to publics. The Westchester Academic Library Directors Organization represents a commitment by a group of academic libraries. In Cyprus, the Near East University Library, with a collection of 1.5 million volumes implemented Koha in 2006.

Evergreen positions itself as scalable to large installations. Its lack of modules for academic reserves, acquisitions, and serials required by academic libraries has so far excluded it from adoption by large academic libraries. The Conifer Project, involving Laurentian University, the University of Windsor, and McMaster University in Canada, has been working on enhancing Evergreen for use in academic libraries, moving toward a target implementation date of May 2009.[12] The University of Prince Edward Island put Evergreen into production in June 2008, using alternate approaches for acquisitions, serials, and course reserves.[13]

Geographic Impact

Open source ILS has made the most significant impact in North America. The United States and Canada provide a more favorable climate for open source ILS than other regions, and the philosophical preference for open source software is stronger in this region. Conferences such as Code4Lib, Access, and the LITA Forums provide fertile venues for cultivating interest in this approach. While open source ILS has made strong inroads into library automation industry in the United States and Canada, its impact elsewhere has been less dramatic.

The United Kingdom, Europe, and Asia have not been so dramatically affected. In these regions, the procurement processes is usually quite formalized. In the recent JISC SCONUL LMS Study report, open source ILS was not portrayed with strong interest:

> The procurement and implementation of an Open Source LMS is not workable for most institutions in the current climate, largely because of the staff capacity and support overheads, but also because the mission criticality of library systems requires users and procurers to have confidence in a robust system. However, Open Source developments are a valuable catalyst for change in terms of exploring possibilities and pushing boundaries for the community.

In the developing world, UNESCO has been very active in distributing various flavors of the CDS/ISIS library automation software to libraries. While some are moving toward open source library automation systems, this is only a small portion of the overall automation efforts in developing countries. In comparison to the thousands of libraries using some variant of the CDS/ISIS software provided by UNESCO, the 122 libraries using NewGenLib is a tiny proportion.[14]

Licensing and Distribution

Each of the open source ILS products covered follows the GNU General Public License for software (see table 8). As we noted above, this is a full copyleft license that ensures strong freedoms in the way that the software is shared and modified. Convenient download sites are provided for Koha, Evergreen, and NewGenLib. Copies of OPALS are provided by Media Flex on request. Most users of OPALS have some kind of relationship with Media Flex, either through a SaaS arrangement or support arrangement.

Commercial Support Firms

Many commercial companies have emerged to promote, support, and develop each of the open source ILS products. While some libraries might venture to implement an open source ILS on their own, the majority seem to prefer working with a specialized vendor for some level of assistance. These companies work with a much different business model than those involved with proprietary ILS products. Their revenue streams are generated exclusively by services rather than by licensing fees (see table 9).

LibLime

The successful deployment of Koha at the Nelsonville Public Library led to interest by other libraries. The library itself could not necessarily commit itself to devote its own resources to assist other libraries with Koha. The individuals involved with the Koha initiative at this library decided to form a separate company devoted to Koha and other open source software for libraries.

LibLime formed in early 2005, with Joshua Ferraro, a former systems administrator at Nelsonville Public Library serving as its CEO. Ryan Higgins served as president for products, and Tina Burger as vice president for marketing.

Since its founding, LibLime has steadily increased its standing as the pivotal company involved with Koha. LibLime operates as a private company, owned by its founders. In 2006, it acquired some assets from Skemotah Solutions, a relatively small endeavor operated by Stephen Hedges, formerly the director of the Nelsonville Public Library. In February 2008 LibLime acquired the Koha-related activates from Katipo Communications, its original developer. LibLime operated this New Zealand operation for about a year until about February 2008[15] Through these acquisitions LibLime gained control of key assets related to Koha, including copyrights, trademarks, and Internet domains, as well as additional customers. In July 2008, LibLime acquired the assets of CARE Affiliates, a firm co-founded by Carl Grant and Lou Leuzzi, specializing in open source software for libraries outside the ILS sphere.

Product	License	Source
Koha	GNU General Public License	www.koha.org/download Koha is written in Perl, so distribution of source code is automatic.
Evergreen	GNU General Public License	http://open-ils.org/downloads.php Includes binaries and source code for Evergreen and OpenSRF
OPALS	GNU General Public License	No download option available; copies of binaries and source code are available from Media Flex on request.
NewGenLib	GNU General Public License	http://sourceforge.net/project/platformdownload.php?group_id=210780

Table 8
Open source ILS license and distribution information

Product	Key Support Company	Brief Background
Koha	LibLime	Launched in early 2005 by individuals involved with the implementation of Koha at the Nelsonville Public Library.
Evergreen	Equinox Software, Inc.	Launched in Jan. 2007 by individuals involved with the creation of Evergreen at the Georgia Public Library System.
OPALS	Media Flex	Veteran company involved in school library automation. Had previously created the Mandarin library automation system. New effort to create a product for this market as open source.
NewGenLib	Kesavan Institute of Information and Knowledge Management / Verus Solutions Pvt. Limited	Developed initially as proprietary software. Made the transition to open source in Jan. 2008.

Table 9
Open source ILS products and companies

Although LibLime gained some assets through these acquisitions, it has primarily seen organic growth through a rapidly growing body of customers with a corresponding increase in staffing. LibLime has attracted a cadre of industry veterans, largely fleeing from other companies, particularly SirsiDynix, which is undergoing downsizing due to recent business consolidations. These have included Galen Charlton, now VP for research and development, formerly with Endeavor Information Systems; John Rose, VP for strategic markets, formerly with SirsiDynix; Marc Roberson, VP for library partners, formerly with SirsiDynix; Debra Denault, operations manager, formerly with VTLS and Ex Libris.[16]

Equinox Software

Development of the Evergreen software for Georgia PINES was done by a team of programmers employed by the Georgia Public Library System. Following the successful implementation of Evergreen for PINES, the team involved with its development broke away from GPLS and formed an independent company named Equinox Software, Inc. The relationship of these individuals relative to SPLS changed from being direct employees to being a private contractor with the state. The development team for Evergreen included Brad LaJeunesse, Jason Etheridge, Mike Rylander, and Bill Erickson, all of whom made the transition from GPLS employees to Equinox Software. LaJeunesse, system administrator for PINES, serves as president of Equinox. GPLS continues to own the majority of the copyrights on Evergreen.

Equinox Software has seen steady growth from its inception. The company has a growing base of customers looking to it to provide support for their use of Evergreen. While still a small company, it has expanded its workforce in tandem with its growing customer base. Industry veterans that have joined Equinox include Robert E. Molyneux, formerly with SirsiDynix; Karen Schneider, well-known writer and blogger; and Shae Tetterton, formerly with SirsiDynix.[17]

Media Flex

Media Flex has long been involved with proving automation products, supplies, and services to libraries. The company primarily focuses on the K–12 school, small college, and special libraries. According to their website, the company was founded in about 1985 by Harry Chan.

The company developed the DOS-based Mandarin library automation system in the mid-1980s. In June 1995, the Mandarin Library Automation System was acquired by SIRS, a publishing company that had previously been a distributor of the Mandarin software in the United States. The DOS-based Mandarin system was superseded by the Windows-based Mandarin M3 system, released in 1998. In 2001, SIRS separated its publishing activities from its library automation division, forming Mandarin Library Automation. At about this time, Chan exited the company and returned to Media Flex, a library supplies and services company that he had also founded. ProQuest acquired SIRS Publishing in July 2003. Mandarin Library Automation continues as an independent company.[18]

Media Flex reentered the library automation industry, developing a new automation system called Open Source Automated Library System, or OPALS, this time following the open source model. Media Flex began development of this system in 2002, targeting much the same type of libraries that used the company's original Mandarin product.

According to the web site, the company operates in the United States under the name Media Flex in Champlain, New York, and internationally from its offices in Montreal, Quebec, under the name Bibliofiche. The company also operates the CERFinfo homework helper site, providing access to over 400,000 Web sites selected for K–12 students and teachers.

CERFinfo
www.cerfinfo.com

Versus Solutions

Though fairly far removed from the North American open source library automation scene, we are seeing a somewhat similar scenario in India. The NewGenLib open source ILS was spearheaded by the Kesavan Institute of Information and Knowledge Management, contracting with Versus Solutions for development and support of the system. Important differences apply to NewGenLib, relative to the North American companies involved in open source ILS. Given the orientation of NewGenLib to libraries in the developing world, opportunities for revenue may not necessarily to sustain the overall venture as a for-profit endeavor.

The original development of NewGenLib followed the proprietary software model. The development of NewGenLib commenced in about 2003, with funding for the development of the system coming from a venture capital firm and from other private sources. The decision to transition the project to open source did not happen until January 2008.[19]

Index Data

Through not offering its own ILS product, no discussion of open source software for libraries would be complete without mentioning Index Data. This company, based in Copenhagen, Denmark, also maintains a presence in the United States and in the United Kingdom. According to their web site, Index Data was co-founded in 1994 by Sebastian Hammer and Adam Dickmeiss. David Dorman serves as the U.S. marketing manager. Sebastian Hammer serves as its president and leads its software development initiatives. Lynn Bailey was appointed as Index Data's CEO in December 2007, and works from Massachusetts. The company employs a total of 10 people.

Index Data has created infrastructure components very widely used in library automation products. Software components created by Index Data are used in the commercial products offered by Ex Libris, Talis, Fretwell-Downing, Infor, Isacsoft, Polaris, and others. Its YAZ toolkit for Z39.50 and SRU/W and server finds use in both proprietary and open source ILS products and is licensed under the Revised BSD license. The YAZ Proxy server, offered under GPL General Public License, can be used in a variety of Z39.50 environments to increase performance and deliver MARC data in XML. Zebra, an XML indexing and retrieval engine, finds broad use, including in Koha and OPALS. The company created a federated search engine it calls Pazpar2 and offers a hosted service version called MasterKey. The open components created by Index Data can be used without cost. The company's business model is based on consulting services and support arrangements surrounding these products and on custom development projects.

Index Data stands as one of the pioneers in the commercial open source arena for library software. Since the company's products tend to be used by other developers, its name may not be as familiar. Still, its impact on the library automation industry cannot be overstated.

Technology Components

Each of the open source ILS products makes use of a number of underlying components. The availability of mature and reliable open source components provides a tremendous advantage available for both open source and proprietary development projects. The use of these components saves developers from reinventing many areas of underlying infrastructure and to focus on the business logic and architecture of their application.

Server Operating System

All of these open source ILS products were designed to run on some flavor of Linux for the server functions. While some might theoretically be able to run under Microsoft Windows Server, libraries interested in using an open source ILS are also likely interested in avoiding proprietary operating systems. But for libraries whose data center might prefer Windows Server, it should be possible to assemble implementations on that platform.

Web Server

The Apache Web is very well established as a Web server and is used in almost all open source Web-based applications and in a large percentage of proprietary products. Each of the open source ILS products uses Apache.

Apache HTTP Server Project
http://httpd.apache.org

Database Engines

The systems make use of different database engines. MySQL, originally developed by MySQL AB and acquired by Sun Microsystems in January 2008 is well established as an open source relational database engine and has the reputation of handling even the largest-scale applications.[20] It offers very fast performance for applications using structured data under a heavy transaction load. Facebook, one of the busiest destinations on the Web, relies on MySQL. Of the open source ILS products under consideration, Koha and OPALS make use of MySQL.

In the library domain, MARC records are notoriously difficult to handle by a standard relational database management systems such as MySQL. One of the issues with early versions of Koha involved concerns with its ability to scale to large-scale use based solely on MySQL. Index Data's Zebra technology offers a scalable data storage and retrieval engine well-suited for MARC and other bibliographic data. LibLime and Index Data collaborated to integrate the Zebra search engine into Koha. It is a standard feature beginning with Version 3.0 for handling the bibliographic database. MySQL continues to power the rest of the system, and for smaller libraries, the system can be configured to use it for the bibliographic database. OPALS follows a similar approach, making use of both MySQL and Zebra.

PostgreSQL is an open source database management environment positioned as the most advanced available, able to handle extremely large and complex data sets and high transaction loads. Evergreen and NewGenLib both rely on PostgreSQL for all data functions.

MySQL
www.mysql.com/

PostgreSQL
www.postgresql.org

Programming Environment

Koha, OPALS, and Evergreen rely on Perl as the programming environment on which their business logic resides. OPALS relies on technologies surrounding Java.

The NewGenLib staff client was created using Java Swing, a programming environment for creating full-featured graphical applications that operate on any platform offering the Java Runtime Environment. Reports and other system features needing text processing rely on Open Office, using the Apache POI libraries for reading and writing files compatible with Microsoft Office. The system makes use of Hibernate to perform mapping between the Java-based business logic and the PostgreSQL database.

Hibernate
www.hibernate.org

Diagram of NewGenLib technology components
www.verussolutions.biz/web/node/18

One of the interesting features of the technology underlying Evergreen involves the Open Scalable Request Framework, or OpenSRF, a communications layer that was created for the project based on the Jabber instant messaging protocol. Jabber implements the Extensible Messaging and Presence Protocol (XMPP), an open, stable and reliable standard. Because the system is based on a service-oriented architecture and designed to be clustered across multiple servers, a messaging layer is required for communications among program elements. What's unusual about Evergreen is that its developers chose to create their own messaging layer rather than use technologies more widely seen in service-oriented applications.

Client Environments

Koha and OPALS rely entirely on the Web for both their online catalog and for staff access to the system. This approach avoids the need to install any software on the computers used by library staff, but means that the software must operate within the limits of what can be accomplished using Web forms, JavaScript, Ajax, and the like. NewGenLib relies on a staff client created in the Java Swing environment, which offers a full graphical interface, but must be installed on staff workstations. The Evergreen staff client is built on XULRunner, an open source runtime environment for building desktop applications created by the Mozilla Foundation. Though based on common Internet technologies, the Evergreen staff client must still be download and installed, but it offers an more sophisticated interface than would be possible through a browser interface alone.

XULRunner
http://developer.mozilla.org/en/XULRunner

These observations on the technology components implemented for each of the systems give us a general impression of the underpinnings each product. All four systems make use of well regarded and widely used components (see table 10). Knowing the technology components involved gives only the most general impression of each system's internal architecture. The ability for each system to withstand the load imposed by a given library depends on a myriad of other factors including issues of systems design, quality of programming, tuning parameters, and the hardware platform selected.

Product	Underlying Components
Koha	**Operating systems supported:** Linux. Debian most common. Windows possible, but less tested **Database:** MySQL for operational data. Zebra from Index Data for bibliographic data. **Programming language:** Perl **Web server:** Apache
Evergreen	**Messaging environment:** OpenSRF (based on Jabber instant messaging protocol) **Database:** PostgreSQL **Programming environment:** Business logic in Perl, infrastructure components in C **Web server:** Apache **Clustering engine:** Slony-I / PGPool **Staff client:** based on XULRunner
OPALS	**Operating system:** Linux **Database:** MySQL, Zebra **Bibliographic search engine:** Zebra from Index Data **Z39.50 engine:** YAZ from Index Data **Web server:** Apache **Programming environment:** Perl
NewGenLib	**Server operating system:** Linux **Web server:** Apache **Database:** PostgreSQL **Java container environment:** Apache Tomcat **Messaging layer:** JDOM (XML-based) Java-based document object model for XML **Object-relational mapping layer:** Hibernate; Apache (formerly Jakarta) POI for reading/writing Microsoft Office files; Open Office **Staff clients:** Java Swing

Table 10
Open source ILS product technology components

Standards

A number of standards, both national and international, have been developed that apply directly to library automation products such as the ILS. The use of these standards ensures that the systems will be interoperable with other automation systems, both those within the organization and those that might be used externally. Standards protect a library's investment in its data, preventing loss of information should the library need to migrate to another system. Table 11 presents a checklist of the standards implemented in each of the open source systems.

Features and Functionality

In this section, we will take a look at the products themselves, looking at the modules offered and some of the general features available in each one. While we attempt to provide some information regarding the functionality of each product, this is not meant to be a definitive review. The observations made derive from live systems, demo sites, or documentation provided by the vendor. The features available will vary according to individual implementations, the version of the software in use, configuration options selected, and the like. Given the nature of open source software to allow local modification, there may be even more local variability than with proprietary systems. While we aim for accuracy, libraries should perform their own assessments of the functionality of systems in which they have an interest.

One of the key differences between a proprietary and an open source ILS involves the accessibility of information about the features available. With proprietary systems, a library may issue an RFP, eliciting a response where the vendor describes the functionality available. With open source systems, libraries can much more easily see the software in action. If they are not able to obtain sufficient information from peer libraries that use the software or from demo systems, they can download and install a copy of the software and even load their own data.

Table 12 identifies the sources that were examined for information presented in this section on the functionality of each system. Tables 13–17 describe only the most basic categories of ILS functionality. They aim to provide only a general impression of the areas of functionality addressed, not necessarily to provide detailed analysis of how a specific function might be implemented and whether it might meet any given library's expectations.

Function	Koha	Evergreen	OPALS	NewGenLib
Unicode 3.0	☑	☑	☑	☑
Z39.50 client	☑	☑	☑	☑
Z39.50 server	☑	☑		⊘
SRU/W server	☑	☑		☑
SRU/W client	☑	☑		⊘
MARC21	☑	☑	☑	☑
ISO 2709 (MARC communications format)	☑	☑	☑	☑
Dublin Core	☑	☑		☑
MODS	☑	☑		☑
OAI-PMH	☑	☑		☑
Z39.71 (serials display)	☑	⊘		☑

Table 11
Standards supported

We do not attempt to compare the functionality of these open source products with the proprietary systems.

The Scope of the ILS

A fundamental trend in libraries is an increased investment in electronic content, especially in collections of electronic journals, aggregated databases of articles, and other packages of content. The ILS has a limited role in the management of this aspect of the library's collection. While the ILS may include bibliographic records for each journal title represented in its electronic collection, it generally does not attempt to provide information about each article within these collections. Libraries license these products from publishers, who usually provide an interface to search and view content from these collections. In its current form, the ILS specializes in the library's print collection.

Given the specialization of the ILS on library print collections, a number of other software products have emerged that deal with different aspects of electronic content. These include:

- **OpenURL link resolvers** for tracking individual holdings within e-journal collections and providing context-sensitive linking. These products maintain a detailed knowledge base of the specific holdings represented by the library's subscriptions to aggregated content packages, e-journals, and other electronic content products.
- **Federated search platforms** simultaneously search multiple resource collections, often including the library catalog and selected packages of electronic content.
- **Electronic resource management systems** specialize in automating the management of the electronic

Product	Sources Consulted
Koha	**Online catalog:** Athens County Public Libraries: http://search.athenscounty.lib.oh.us **Staff client:** http://academic-staff.demo.kohalibrary.com
Evergreen	**Online catalog:** Georgia PINES: http://gapines.org **Staff client:** Downloaded and installed staff client from: http://demo.gapines.org and used demo library login.
OPALS	**Online catalog:** http://opalsbtl.stier.org/bin/home **Staff client:** Documentation and screen images from http://www.opals-na.org
NewGenLib	**Online catalog:** Bangalore University: http://202.141.128.115:8080/newgenlibctxt/LibraryAction.do?college=Bangalore%20University%20Library **Staff functionality:** NewGenLib website: www.newgenlib.com

Table 12
Open source ILS products: sources of information on functionality

content product subscriptions, including aspects of procurement, license tracking, access rights, vendor contact data, usage reporting, and other information to help the library efficiently manage its electronic collections.
- **Discovery interfaces** provide an alternative to the online catalog module delivered with an ILS. This genre of products aims to provide access to a broader range of resources beyond that managed within the ILS, following interface techniques consistent with modern Web destinations such as faceted browsing, relevance-ranked results, visually enhanced displays, and advanced resource fulfillment services.

We are starting to see movement toward a more comprehensive approach to automation beyond these traditional limits. The Open Library Environment (OLE) project has recently launched as a multi-institutional effort. Led by Duke University with funding from the Andrew W. Mellon Foundation, this project is working toward the development a more expansive model of library automation based on the Service Oriented Architecture and vendor initiatives, such as Universal Resource Management system articulated by Ex Libris.

Please note that the open source ILS products considered in this report largely stay within the confines of the traditional scope as established by their proprietary counterparts.

Open Library Environment (OLE) project
http://oleproject.org

Support for Consortia

Libraries follow many different organizational models that have a major impact on the way that they implement their automation environment. Some libraries operate fairly independently and correspondingly want their own ILS to manage and provide access to its resources. It's extremely common, however, for libraries to be organized into consortia and to share an implementation of an ILS. A consortial implementation of an ILS allows the participating libraries to pool their resources to lower the costs associated with systems management. More important, by combining their collections they offer more materials for their users.

Providing support for a consortium introduces a number of challenges for the ILS. Creating an ILS for a single library involves support for a simpler organization structure. Consortia involve more complex organizations of participating libraries. A key challenge of an ILS used to automate a consortium involves balancing the needs for the individual libraries to maintain their identities and local automation preferences versus gaining efficiencies through sharing resources and policies across the consortium as a whole. ILS implementations for consortia must manage much larger collections and must stand up to very high transaction loads to accommodate the combined automation activities of each participating library.

Evergreen positions itself as an open source ILS designed to accommodate consortia. Its initial development for a large consortium of public libraries in Georgia reinforces this capability. The system allows each library the ability to define its individual policies and preferences for circulation while providing a high degree of resource sharing through a shared consortial catalog.

OPALS was also designed to provide a high level of resource sharing for school libraries through union catalogs, district-wide implementations, and consortia of school districts. The implementations of OPALS in several BOCES in New York demonstrate the system's ability to support the complexity and performance requirements of large consortial implementations.

Koha has also seen a number of consortial implementations, including the MassCat in Massachusetts, several regional library systems in Kansas, and the Indiana Shared Catalog. In addition to consortial implementations, many Koha implementations support single library organizations, many including multiple branches or facilities.

Online Catalog

The online catalog module, sometimes called the online public access catalog (OPAC) of the ILS, enables users to search the library's collections and take advantage of online services. Basic functionality of this module includes the ability for users to perform searches or browse through the collection and to view descriptive and status information on any given item. Most ILS online catalogs allow patrons to sign into a personal account, view lists of items that they have currently checked out, renew items, place requests for items, pay outstanding fines, and other similar services.

Traditionally this component of the system has focused on access to print collections; as libraries transition to managing increasing proportions of electronic content, the role of the online catalog has become more complex. Many libraries, for example, have implemented products from a new breed of discovery interfaces that aim to provide access to a broader universe of content beyond that managed by the ILS.

The interfaces expressed in Koha and Evergreen bear many similarities to the standalone discovery interface products. They look more modern, make use of faceted browsing, default to relevance sorting of results, and makes use of cover art to enhance the visual appeal of the user

Function	Koha	Evergreen	OPALS	NewGenLib
Basic search (single search box)	☑	☑	☑	☑
Advanced search (multiple field selections)	☑	☑	☑	☑
Brief display list	☑	☑	☑	☑
Full record display	☑	☑	☑	☑
MARC display	☑	☑	☑	⊘
Faceted browsing	☑	☑	⊘	☑
Relevancy sorting	☑	☑	⊘	☑
Book jacket display	☑	☑	☑	⊘
Download / save records	☑	☑	☑	☑
E-mail records	☑	⊘		☑
Place / cancel hold (or reservations)	☑	☑		☑
Shelf / call number browse	☑	☑		⊘
Browse collection (author, title, series)	⊘	☑	☑	☑
Patron login	☑	☑	☑	☑
Patron account—view item charged to me	☑	☑	☑	☑
Patron account—pay fines	⊘	☑		☑
RSS delivery of search results	☑	⊘	⊘	⊘
Integrated federated search	☑	⊘	☑	⊘

Table 13
Online catalog functionality checklist

interface. NewGenLib and OPALS offer online catalogs with much more traditional interface design (see table 13).

Circulation

The circulation module of the ILS addresses a need every library has—to automate the tasks involved in loaning materials to library patrons. This module must offer very simple and efficient ways to perform routine transactions like checkouts, renewals, and returns. The circulation module uses the databases that manage the items within the collection and registered library patrons and often includes the ability to create new records when records are not already present in the system. Many libraries impose fines when materials are not returned on schedule, requiring the circulation module to track fine accumulations, manage payments, produce notices, and perform related functions. Requirements for circulation features vary by library type. Academic libraries, for example, often need the ability to manage a collection of items placed on reserve for courses, imposing in-house or short-term loans during the term of a course. Public libraries must deal with much heavier volumes of circulation transactions.

Each of the open source ILS products has quite capable circulation features, especially for public library environments. Academic reserves are currently under development for Evergreen and Koha (see table 14).

Cataloging

Any ILS must provide users with the ability to create records for new additions to the collection. A common workflow involves retrieving records from external resources such as OCLC WorldCat, the Library of Congress, or other libraries when possible, using a utility based on the Z39.50 search and retrieval protocol. When no existing record can be found, the cataloging utility needs to support the creation of original records. The library profession has well-established standards such as MARC21 and AACR2 to ensure that bibliographic records can be exchanged among libraries and that each field within the record will be populated consistently. Professional-level cataloging also involves the use of authority files to ensure the consistent use of names and subject headings.

The cataloging module also addresses the physical processing of materials, such as the creation of spine labels or pocket labels (see table 15).

Function	Koha	Evergreen	OPALS	NewGenLib
Check item to patron	☑	☑	☑	☑
Check in item	☑	☑	☑	☑
Register new patrons	☑	☑	☑	☑
Renew Items	☑	☑	☑	☑
Assess fines for late return	☑	☑	☑	☑
Fine notices	☑	☑	☑	⊘
Place items on hold (reserve)	☑	☑	☑	☑
Tally in-house use	☑	☑	☑	☑
Circulation of noncataloged items	☑	☑	☑	⊘
Academic course reserves (short-term loans)	⊘	⊘	⊘	☑

Table 14
Circulation functionality checklist

Acquisitions

The acquisitions module provides support—mostly on the financial side—for the process of adding new items to library collections. This module usually involves a database from each of the vendors that the library uses to purchase new materials and a financial system for tracking and allocating funds according to various budget categories. There are specific tasks automated by the acquisitions module, including placing firm orders for a needed item, managing approval plans where vendors supply materials based on collection criteria, processing invoices for items received, and approving payments. Larger libraries may implement automated transfer of data with their large suppliers, using protocols such as EDI.

The acquisitions process is one of the most complex aspects of library automation. Large libraries tend to make extensive use of the acquisitions functionality, often involving complex interchange of data with other financial systems. Smaller libraries may not use this module at all, managing the procurement of items by using spreadsheets. Academic libraries, especially large ones, tend to rely heavily on the ILS for the financial management of their collections budgets.

Development of an acquisitions module is underway for Evergreen. The next major release, Evergreen Version 2, has been positioned as the academic release, including modules for academic reserves, acquisitions, and serials management (see table 16).

Function	Koha	Evergreen	OPALS	NewGenLib
Create bibliographic / title-level record	☑	☑	☑	☑
Simple template for record creation	☑	☑	☑	☑
Support for MARC 21	☑	☑	☑	☑
Import MARC records with Z39.50	☑	☑	☑	☑
Add volumes / holdings / items	☑	☑	☑	☑
Harvest records with OAI-PMH	⊘	⊘	⊘	☑
Authority control	☑	☑	☑	☑
Produce spine labels	☑	☑	☑	☑
Produce pocket labels	☑	☑	☑	⊘
Export MARC records	☑	☑	☑	☑
MARC record validation	☑	☑	☑	⊘
Built-in documentation for MARC	☑	☑	☑	☑

Table 15
Cataloging functionality checklist

Function	Koha	Evergreen	OPALS	NewGenLib
Fund management	☑	○	○	☑
Vendor file	☑	○	○	☑
Place firm orders	☑	○	○	☑
Receive orders	☑	○	○	☑
Invoice processing (manual)	☑	○	○	☑
Invoice processing (EDI)	○	○	○	○
Approve / process payments	☑	○	○	☑
Claim items not received on time	☑	○	○	☑
Patron-initiated requests	☑	○	○	☑
Staff approval of patron requests	☑	○	○	☑
Gifts processing	☑	○	○	☑

Table 16
Acquisitions functionality checklist

Serials Control

The management of books seems simple compared to of the process of managing periodicals and other serials. Dealing with these materials involves both an initial establishment of a subscription and ongoing tasks related to incoming issues or volumes. The subscription record needs to reflect the expected schedule of the delivery of issues, the length of the subscription term, and other details. Given the great variability in the publication of serials, tracking them can get quite complex. Some of the tasks associated with the serials module include checking in issues as they arrive, generating claims for issues expected but not received and creating summarized holdings as issues are bound into volumes. The serials module manages the process of renewing the library's roster of subscriptions, often handled in bulk in conjunction with a serials subscription agent. Given the complexity of the materials involved, serials modules involve specialized and nuanced functionality.

One of the major issues in recent times, as libraries increasingly shift from print to electronic serials, involves the overlap between the serials module, the OpenURL link resolver, and an electronic resources management system. In the context of this trend toward electronic content, the need for the serials module of the ILS diminishes as the demand for an electronic resource management system increases.

The development of acquisitions and serials modules typically follows the basic modules like cataloging, circulation, and the online catalog. Some types of libraries, such as those in schools, tend not to use these modules, and even the fully mature ILS products geared toward them may not incorporate these modules (see table 17).

In broad terms, the functionality of the open source ILS products has matured at a fast pace. As more libraries adopt the software and choose to sponsor specific development projects, any lapses in functionality seem to be closing rapidly. Nevertheless, any library considering

Function	Koha	Evergreen	OPALS	NewGenLib
Create subscription record	☑	○	○	☑
Modify subscription	☑	○	○	☑
Checkin issues	☑	○	○	☑
Generate claims for missing / late issues	☑	○	○	☑
Binding management	○	○	○	☑
Support for MARC-21 format for holdings	○	○	○	☑

Table 17
Serials control functionality checklist

adopting an open source ILS needs to carefully review the features and functionality currently available and measure those against its current and anticipated needs.

It would be unrealistic, however, to suggest that the current open source ILS products can match the needs of the world's largest and most complex libraries. Many large academic libraries that express a high degree of motivation to move to an open source ILS have yet to migrate to one of these systems. It seems almost inevitable that the level of functionality will continually increase, broadening the universe of libraries for which an open source ILS will be a viable option.

Note

1. Many of the details of the implementation of Koha have been chronicled in "A koha Dairy: implementing Koha at the Nelsonville Public Library" by Stephen Hedges. http://www.kohadocs.org/koha_diary.html.
2. Based on personal correspondence with library director Stephen Hedges.
3. See the Georgia Public Library Service PINES Web site: http://www.georgialibraries.org/public/pines.php
4. Sirsi Corporation press relsease: http://www.librarytechnology.org/ltg-displaytext.pl?RC=8908
5. Text of the letter is available: http://www.librarytechnology.org/ltg-displaytext.pl?RC=10943
6. Breeding, Marshall. "PINES sets precedent for open source ILS" Smart Libraries Newsletter. ALA TechSource October 2006. p. 1
7. See: http://eboces.wnyric.org/wps/portal/BOCESofNYS
8. Pushpinder, K. Gill. "The State of Open Source Software in North Carolina School Media Centers" A master's paper for the M.S. in Library Science degree. July 2004. p. 23
9. Breeding, Marshall. "NewGenLib: An open source ILS for Libraries." Smart Libraries Newsletter. ALA TechSource. March 2008. p. 3.
10. See http://dbl.gov.in
11. Data from lib-web-cats http://www.librarytechnology.org
12. See: http://conifer.mcmaster.ca/
13. See Equinox Software press release: http://www.librarytechnology.org/ltg-displaytext.pl?RC=13302; Breeding, Marshall. "Evergreen Expands into Academic" Smart Libraries Newsletter. ALA TechSource. July 2008. p. 1-3.
14. See: http://www.verussolutions.biz/web/node/24
15. Based on personal correspondence with LibLime officials.
16. See LibLime press release "LibLime to Acquire CARE Affiliates" July 28, 2008. http://www.librarytechnology.org/ltg-displaytext.pl?RC=13424
17. Based on Equinox Software press releases
18. See Breeding, Marshall. "Partial management buyout at Mandarin." Smart Libraries Newsletter. ALA TechSource. October 2007.
19. See http://www.kiikm.org/. Also based on personal correspondence with L. J. Haravu.
20. See MySQL press release: http://www.mysql.com/news-and-events/sun-to-acquire-mysql.html
21. Veronica Adamson et al., *JISC & SCONUL Library Management Systems Study*, March 2008, 9. www.jisc.ac.uk/media/documents/programmes/resourcediscovery/lmsstudy.pdf (accessed Sept. 23, 2008)

Chapter 4

Conclusions and Observations

The new developments in the open source ILS arena show a group of products offering respectable functionality for libraries. While not suitable for all types and sizes of libraries, there are viable alternatives to specific sectors of the library automation market. It's not a panacea—open source ILS products and the companies that support them include both strengths and weaknesses that warrant objective consideration.

We're past the pioneering days of open source library automation. The realm of open source ILS products no longer belongs only to libraries with advanced technology resources. There are only a small minority of libraries that take on open source ILS implementations completely on their own. The majority of libraries selecting an open source ILS opt to work with a company that provides a complete set of implementation and support services. Though early in the market adoption cycle, open source ILSs are well within the mainstream of the library automation industry.

The emergence of open source ILS products and the companies that create them or provide support has altered the dynamics of the library automation industry. We can expect an increasing number of libraries to move to open source ILS support models. Some of the vendors offering proprietary systems have not necessarily delivered products and service that meet basic expectations or have failed to maintain the trust and confidence of their library customers; they stand vulnerable to the rising open source ILS movement. However, it is still too soon too see how much this movement will encroach on the dominance of the companies that develop and support proprietary ILS products. Many of these products and companies have delivered highly capable systems, offer high-caliber support, and have earned the loyalty of their library customers.

This report provides basic information that libraries need as they consider their ILS options. A library performing a thorough consideration of a new ILS should examine both open source and proprietary options. This report has focused only on the open source ILS. A thorough process of evaluating an ILS today would not be complete without also weighing the open source ILS products against their proprietary counterparts.

This report provides a snapshot in time of the open source ILS products and companies. The world of ILS is evolving rapidly, even more so than previous trends in library technology. It is possible that new open source ILS products may emerge and new companies will enter the scene. The current products will evolve. The products and companies offering proprietary ILS products will respond to the challenges offered by the open source movement. At the same time, the basic concept of the ILS is changing, fueling new rounds of competition between open source and proprietary products.